Brands We Know

Coca-Cola

By Sara Green

Bellwether Media • Minneapolis, MN

Jump into the cockpit and take flight with *Pilot* books. Your journey will take you on high-energy adventures as you learn about all that is wild, weird, fascinating, and fun!

This edition first published in 2016 by Bellwether Media, Inc.

No part of this publication may be reproduced in whole or in part without written permission of the publisher.
For information regarding permission, write to Bellwether Media, Inc.,
Attention: Permissions Department,
5357 Penn Avenue South, Minneapolis, MN 55419.

Library of Congress Cataloging-in-Publication Data

Green, Sara, 1964- author.
 Coca-Cola / by Sara Green.
     pages cm -- (Pilot. Brands We Know)
  Summary: "Engaging images accompany information about the
Coca-Cola Company. The combination of high-interest subject matter
and narrative text is intended for students in grades 3 through 7"--
Provided by publisher.
  Audience: Ages 7-12
  Audience: Grades 3 to 7
  Includes bibliographical references and index.
  ISBN 978-1-62617-287-6 (hardcover: alk. paper)
 1. Coca-Cola Company--History--Juvenile literature. 2. Soft drink
industry--United States--History--Juvenile literature. I. Title. II. Series:
Green, Sara, 1964- Brands We Know. III. Series: Pilot (Bellwether Media)
  HD9349.S634G74 2016
  338.7'663620973--dc23
                     2015005568

Printed in the United States of America, North Mankato, MN.

Table of Contents

What Is Coca-Cola?

More than 100 years ago, a Georgia drugstore **soda fountain** made history. There, Coca-Cola was poured into glasses for the first time. People found the sweet, refreshing soda to be delightful. Today, Coca-Cola is still popular. Coke, Diet Coke, Sprite, Fanta, and other favorite Coca-Cola drinks are enjoyed in almost every country on the planet.

The Coca-Cola Company is the world's largest **beverage** company. It owns more than 500 **brands**. The company **headquarters** is in Atlanta, Georgia. Today, Coca-Cola is one of the most recognized brands in the world. It is also among the most valuable. In 2015, the company was worth nearly $180 billion.

By the Numbers

more than
3,500
products sold
worldwide

more than
700,000
employees
worldwide

more than
1.9 billion
beverage servings
sold each day

more than
**79 billion gallons
(299 billion liters)**
of water added to
Coke syrup each year

94%
percent of the world's
population recognizes
the Coca-Cola logo

John Pemberton's Tonic

In 1886, Dr. John Pemberton invented Coca-Cola in Atlanta, Georgia. John was a **pharmacist**. He wanted to create a headache medicine. Working in the back of his shop, John mixed many ingredients together. These included parts of the kola nut and coca leaf. John heated and stirred the ingredients. The result was a sticky brown syrup called a **tonic**.

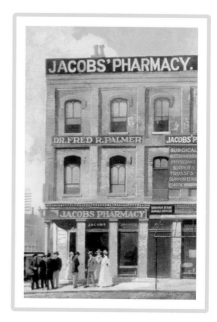

John took the tonic to Jacobs' Pharmacy, a drugstore in Atlanta. There, it was mixed with **carbonated** water. The manager sold it at the soda fountain. Customers loved the fizzy drink! It sold for five cents a glass. John's business partner, Frank Robinson, suggested a name for the new drink. He combined the two special ingredient names into Coca-Cola. Then, he wrote the name in flowing handwriting. In time, Frank's writing became the company's **logo**.

Coca-Cola

Dr. John Pemberton

**Around the Corner
from Everywhere**

1920s tagline

A Slow Start
The first year, John Pemberton
sold around nine servings
of Coca-Cola a day. His total
earnings were about $50.

The Coca-Cola Company

John was proud of Coca-Cola. But he decided to pursue other ideas. He began to sell his **shares** of the company. Many of them were sold to businessman Asa Candler. In 1888, Asa bought up the remaining Coca-Cola shares. In 1892, he formed The Coca-Cola Company. Asa wanted to make Coca-Cola even more popular. He gave out thousands of coupons for free drinks. He also **advertised** Coca-Cola on posters, calendars, clocks, and other items. Sales of Coca-Cola rose quickly. Asa opened new syrup plants in Texas, Illinois, and California. By 1895, Coca-Cola was being sold all across the United States.

Asa Candler

Delicious and Refreshing

1900s-1920s tagline

Coca-Cola bottling plant in North Carolina

EVERY BOTTLE STERILIZED

What A Bargain
Lawyers Benjamin Thomas and Joseph Whitehead of Tennessee bought the rights to bottle Coca-Cola for $1. A third lawyer joined their business soon after.

People enjoyed drinking Coca-Cola at soda fountains. But many wanted to drink it at home. In 1899, with Asa's permission, three lawyers from Tennessee started to bottle Coca-Cola. The demand for bottles of Coke rose quickly. The three men could not keep up. They decided to sell bottling **rights** to others. By 1909, there were nearly 400 Coca-Cola bottling plants.

Sales of Coca-Cola continued to climb. Soon, Coca-Cola bottlers faced a problem. Other people were making similar products and bottles. Coca-Cola needed to stand out. In 1915, an Indiana glass company designed a new Coca-Cola bottle. It had the curvy shape of a cocoa pod. This bottle would become one of the most recognized packages on Earth.

By 1920, Coca-Cola was being bottled in more than 1,000 plants in the United States. The company also added new plants overseas during World War II to provide Coke to soldiers.

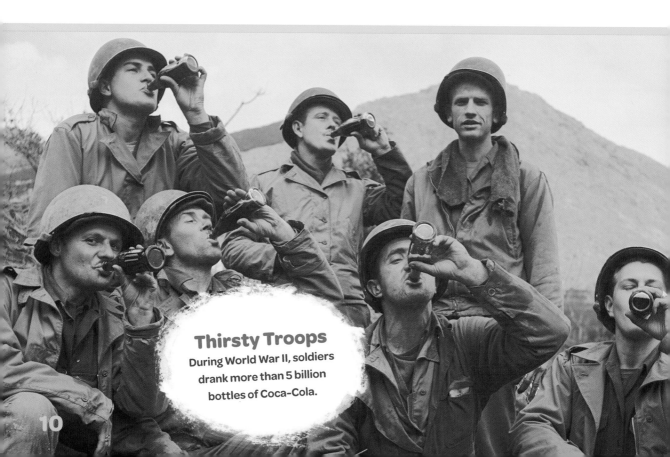

Thirsty Troops
During World War II, soldiers drank more than 5 billion bottles of Coca-Cola.

Coke Bottles
Through the Years

| 1899 | 1900 | 1916 | 1957 | 1961 | 1991 | 1993 | 2007 |

Coca-Cola ... Along the Highway to Anywhere

1940s tagline

The late twentieth century brought changes to the product line. Around 1960, people were able to buy Coca-Cola in cans. The 1960s also introduced products other than Coke. Fanta, Sprite, TaB, and Fresca appeared in the United States. People loved these new soft drinks! Mr. PiBB and Mello Yello were introduced in the 1970s. In 1982, Diet Coke came on the market. It soon became the top-selling diet soda in the world.

Serving Up Smiles

The Coca-Cola Company has achieved great success. But it has also experienced failure. In 1985, the company made a huge mistake. That year, it changed the original Coca-Cola recipe to make it sweeter. The result was known as New Coke. Many customers were unhappy and refused to buy New Coke. They wanted the original Coca-Cola back. In response, the company brought back the original **formula** as Coca-Cola Classic. It eventually stopped making New Coke. Coca-Cola fans were overjoyed. Sales of the soft drink became strong again. Today, Coca-Cola is the most popular soft drink in the world.

Jolly St. Nick

In 1931, Haddon Sundblom created an ad showing Santa Claus drinking a Coke. His illustration helped shape the modern image of Santa Claus.

Coca-Cola has gained customers through creative advertising. A 1993 commercial introduced cuddly polar bears as beloved **mascots**. Catchy Coca-Cola **jingles** have become radio hits. Much of Coca-Cola's advertising focuses on friendship, fun, and happiness. It features people enjoying good times together while they drink Coca-Cola. They find Coca-Cola delicious and refreshing!

Over time, people's concerns about **obesity** and other health risks have increased. Many people have cut back on sugary soft drinks. To keep profits high, The Coca-Cola Company bought other beverage brands. Today, the company owns Simply and Minute Maid, which are famous for their juices. It also owns Dasani bottled water and Powerade sports drinks. Odwalla, another Coca-Cola brand, is known for its juices and smoothies. One of its newest brands is called Fairlife. This company makes milk.

Simply

Minute Maid

Dasani

Powerade

Odwalla

Fairlife

A Coca-Cola Attraction

A vault in the World of Coca-Cola museum in Atlanta, Georgia, contains Coca-Cola's secret formula. Only a few top Coca-Cola leaders are ever allowed to see it.

stevia

The Coca-Cola Company also added low-calorie soft drinks. Diet Coke and Coca-Cola Zero both have zero calories. However, Coca-Cola Zero was made to have the original Coke flavor. In 2013, The Coca-Cola Company introduced a soft drink called Coca-Cola Life. It is made with **stevia**, a natural sweetener. This means that the drink has less sugar. With so many choices available, Coca-Cola is sure to have a beverage for every person's taste!

A World of Flavors

Every day, nearly 2 billion servings of Coca-Cola beverages are enjoyed around the world. In most countries, people can find Coca-Cola, Diet Coke, Sprite, and other favorites. However, different cultures have unique taste preferences. For this reason, Coca-Cola does not sell the same beverages in every country. For example, in the United Kingdom, people enjoy a juice drink called Oasis. Flavors include black currant apple and mixed berry. A favorite drink in South Africa is Twist. Its flavors include lemon and mango. Tiky is a popular soft drink in Guatemala. It tastes like pineapple!

People can try new beverage flavors with Coca-Cola Freestyle. These soda machines are found in places such as restaurants and movie theaters. They offer more than 100 drink choices. People first select a beverage using the touch screen. Next, they choose a flavor, such as orange, raspberry, or vanilla. People love trying orange Coke, peach Sprite, and other delicious flavors!

Coca-Cola Brands Around the World

Brand Name	Country of Origin	What Is It?
Ambasa	Japan	Milk-flavored soft drink
Bistrone	Japan	Soup
Café Zu	Thailand	Canned coffee
Ciel	Mexico	Bottled water
Del Valle	Mexico	Juice
Dorna	Romania	Carbonated mineral water
Eight O'Clock	Philippines	Juice drink
Far Coast	Canada	Coffee and tea
Ice Dew	China	Bottled water
Lemon & Paeroa	New Zealand	Soft drink
Olimpija	Bosnia & Herzegovina	Mineral water
Powerplay	South Africa	Energy drink
Samurai	Vietnam	Energy drink
Ten Ren	Taiwan	Tea

Café Zu

Ciel

Far Coast

Powerplay

Samurai

Spreading Happiness

The Coca-Cola Company has a long history of **philanthropy**. Asa Candler and other Coca-Cola leaders were known for their generosity. Their donations have helped many universities, community groups, and hospitals.

In 1984, The Coca-Cola Company started The Coca-Cola **Foundation**. It has given more than $650 million to projects all over the world. Many projects focus on protecting the environment. Some seek to improve education and health care. The foundation's projects often change people's lives forever. One has given many people in Africa access to safe drinking water. Other projects support community **conservation** and recycling programs. These include planting trees in Mexico and cleaning rivers in Tanzania.

Protecting Polar Bears

Polar bear homes are melting around the world. Coca-Cola is working with the World Wildlife Fund to help the bears. They plan to raise $10 million to save their beloved mascots' home.

drinking water
in Africa

The Coca-Cola Company also supports a program called 5by20. Its goal is to help five million women succeed in business by the year 2020. The Coca-Cola Company continues to spread happiness through delicious beverages and projects that care for our world.

Coca-Cola Timeline

1886
Dr. John Pemberton creates Coca-Cola

1892
Asa Candler creates The Coca-Cola Company

1923
Coca-Cola begins using the six-bottle carton

1928
Coca-Cola sponsors the Olympic Games in Amsterdam

1915
The contour bottle is designed

1899
The rights to bottle Coca-Cola are sold

1919
Ernest Woodruff and a group of investors buy The Coca-Cola Company from the Candler family for $25 million

1886
Frank Robinson names the drink "Coca-Cola" and creates the logo

1906
Coca-Cola bottling operations begin in Cuba, Panama, and Canada

1945
"Coke" becomes a trademark of The Coca-Cola Company

1950
Coca-Cola is the first product to appear on the cover of *Time* magazine

1965
Coca-Cola sponsors the first broadcast of *A Charlie Brown Christmas*

2009
Coca-Cola introduces Coca-Cola Freestyle

1960
Coca-Cola first comes in cans

1982
Diet Coke is introduced

2000
Coca-Cola is named the World's Most Valuable Brand

1961
Sprite is introduced

2005
Coca-Cola Zero is introduced

1971
The famous television commercial "I'd Like to Buy the World a Coke" airs

1993
Coca-Cola polar bears appear in the "Northern Lights" television commercial

1950
The first television commercial for Coca-Cola airs on Thanksgiving Day

Glossary

advertised—announced or promoted something to get people to buy it

beverage—something you can drink

brands—categories of products all made by the same company

carbonated—fizzy due to the addition of carbon dioxide

conservation—the protection of animals, plants, and natural resources

formula—recipe

foundation—an institution that provides funds to charitable organizations

headquarters—a company's main office

jingles—short, memorable songs used to promote things

logo—a symbol or design that identifies a brand or product

mascots—animals or objects used as symbols by a group or company

obesity—being extremely overweight

pharmacist—a person who prepares and gives out prescription medication

philanthropy—giving time and money to help others

rights—the legal ability to use a certain name or product

shares—units of ownership of a company

soda fountain—a shop or counter where drinks, ice cream, and occasionally light meals were sold

stevia—a shrub whose leaves are used to make a sweetener

tonic—a medicine used to increase energy and well-being

To Learn More

AT THE LIBRARY

Bodden, Valerie. *The Story of Coca-Cola*. Mankato, Minn.:
Creative Education, 2009.

Griffin Llanas, Sheila. *Caleb Davis Bradham: Pepsi-Cola Inventor*.
Edina, Minn.: Abdo Publishing, 2015.

Griffin Llanas, Sheila. *John Pemberton: Coca-Cola Developer*.
Edina, Minn.: Abdo Publishing, 2015.

ON THE WEB

Learning more about Coca-Cola
is as easy as 1, 2, 3.

1. Go to www.factsurfer.com.

2. Enter "Coca-Cola" into the search box.

3. Click the "Surf" button and you
   will see a list of related web sites.

With factsurfer.com, finding more information
is just a click away.

Index

The images in this book are reproduced through the courtesy of: M. Unal Ozmen, front cover (cup), p. 4 (Coke); Coca-Cola, front cover (Minute Maid drops, Dasani drops, Powerade, Vitamin Water, polar bear, Hi-C), Table of Contents (Coca-Cola logo), pp. 6 (bottom), 7, 8 (left, right), 11, 12 (bottom), 13, 14 (Simply left, Simply right, Minute Maid left, Minute Maid right, Dasani left, Dasani right, Powerade left, Powerade right, Odwalla left, Odwalla right), 15 (top), 17 (Café Zu, Ciel, Far Coast, Powerplay, Samurai), 19, 20 (top, bottom), 21 (top right, bottom); Lunasee Studios, front cover (six-pack); Twin Design, front cover (Coca-Cola Zero); Yuri Samsonov, front cover (Sprite, Coca-Cola bottle, Fanta); Popartic, front cover (Coca-Cola logo, bottle cap), p. 4 (Sprite, Fanta); Jag_cz, front cover (background drops); Evdokimov Maxim, p. 5, John Van Hasselt/ Corbis, p. 6 (top); Underwood & Underwood/ Corbis, p. 9; Sherman Montrose/ Corbis, p. 10; Al Freni/ Getty Images, p. 12 (top); Bellwether Media, pp. 14 (Fairlife), 16; Chones, p. 15 (Diet Coke, Coca-Cola Zero); dean bertoncelj, p. 15 (Coca-Cola Life); Swapan Photography, p. 15 (stevia); Tripplaar Kristoffer/ SIPA/ Newscom, p. 18; Handout/ KRT/ Newscom, p. 21 (top left).